In-Between Times:

Informative, Inspirational and Motivational Poetry

Written by: Charles Antonio Parham

Part I

Dedications

I would like to dedicate this book to Jesus Christ, God Almighty for blessing me with my creative talents. Everything that I am is because of you. You are a light unto me when I'm in darkness. You helped me see that I am more than a painter, sculptor, designer, but a poet. This book belongs to you.

To the late Charlie R. Parham and Shirley D. Parham. Thank you for your guidance. You are truly missed from the depths of my heart. Thank you for your encouraging words in my adversity and tribulations. I will always keep them in my heart.

To my Leader, Teacher, Guide and General overseer Pastor Gino Jennings. Thank you for the spiritual training needed to survive in life. May God Almighty Bless you with a long life of health and strength. Keeping preaching hard!

To Drs. Kerry James Evans and Bill Ndi for your words of wisdom in writing poetry.

Copyright © by Charles Antonio Parham

All rights reserved. No part of this book may be reproduced or transmitted in any form or by any means without written permission from the Author or Publisher.

Published by: Ware Resources and Publishing
www.wareresources.com

1-888-469-4850 Ext. 2

ISBN 979-8-9859685-2-1

L.C.C.N: 2022908913

Printed in USA by Ware Resources and Publishing

Table of Contents

8. A message from the author
9. Beast
10. Carcinogen Personality
11. I am carved from fire
12. Clogged Arteries: A Self-Portrait
13. Drowning your talent
14. Nightmare
15. Ears
16. Coneheads
17. Wormwood and Gall
18. Failure
19. False Accusers
20. Famine
21. Fire
22. Forgiveness
23. Grave Diggers
24. Grip
25. Hidden Agenda: A message to the gullible
26. I will arise
27. In the midst of fire
28. Isolated
29. Jewels
30. Gun Ptah

31. A cold heart
32. Swallow Your Pride
33. Light equals knowledge
34. A smile
35. Nay-sayers
36. Pig slop
37. Chained Down
38. Reckless energy
39. Regret
40. Remote control
41. Revenge
42. Revolving Door
43. Sinister Zeitgeist
44. Someday the stone will roll away
45. Werewolves
46. Star Gazer
47. Stepping stones- A Homage to Coach Rock
48. People are not sincere
49. Taking a stand for truth
50. The Abyss

A Message from the Author

In-Between Times are the space of time between birth and death. It is a time where experimentation, exploration, joy, hardships, lost and adversities abide. *In-Between Times* is also a time when your patience is put to the test. It reveals how much or little you can endure. It is the ultimate mirror that reflects the real you. In my *In-Between Times*, I suffered a lot of adversity which I am currently dealing with, but through it all my faith in Jesus Christ sustains me and gives me hope that my breakthrough is near.

First, my faith showed me how to cope with my *In-Between Times*. In them, I discovered poetry. This may not be the case with you, but it is a possibility that you could find another route that is pure and positive that can sustain you during your *In-Between Times*. I am saying this because I am only a speck of dust in this atmosphere that breathes air just like you, so if I can do it you can do the same. Secondly, I do not know your circumstance at this moment. Some of you may be experiencing similar situations as I am experiencing or some of you may be dealing with much more than what I am dealing with, but if you are I am here to show you that there is hope. Lastly, I do hope this collection of informative, inspirational and motivational poetry will be a motivation for you and your generations after you.

In closing, I hope that you take comfort in these poems to get you through your *In-Between Times* like they are doing for me. Stay encouraged and keep your vision a burning desire.

Peace be unto you,

Charles Antonio Parham

Beast

I received my graduate degree in hopes of finding a job after graduation.

My hopes were in vain. A $10 an hour security job sustained me until an

opportunity was waiting for the right time to blossom. Almost 2 years passed

before I got the job. My frustration grew into a cankerous sore inside the mouth.

I became bitter and all I could think about was student loan debt.

Debt covered me like I was underwater, but I manage to stay afloat.

My faith and patience were in my favor. A phone call from a dear friend brought

joy inside of me. He informed me that I was hired as a college professor. I was only

27 years old. What an achievement. It was similar to a law student

who just heard they passed the Bar Exam. A small HBCU (Historical black college/university)

in Georgia provided me a platform to express the knowledge that I learned to help inspire future artists.

In unknown territory, I was a novice in a wilderness of wolves.

I was not privy on how to recognize shapeshifters. My inexperience would later cause me

great pain. Jealously and envy were sharp teeth that sunk its teeth in my body.

My ambition and determination exposed their laziness as educators. As a wolf stalks his prey,

a shapeshifter composed strategies on how to get rid of me. They gave me a project that I was unfamiliar

with hoping they could use this as leverage not to renew my letter of agreement. Their hopes were in vain.

There is power in prayer. The night before the project, I knelt down on the side of my bed and asked GOD to help guide me through the project. My prayer was answered. A two-week project was completed in one week.

This pushed his skullduggery into overdrive. He had to get rid of me. On a hot Friday in July my phone ranges and

my supervisor announced that I was no longer needed in the department.

I got positive reviews on my performance evaluations, I just purchased a home, I never missed a day of work and I

had plans in seeking a wife for the future of my progeny. With all of these good qualities how could they release me I thought?

A false colleague who pretenced that he cared feared that his job was in jeopardy.

He painted a picture of me as being violent and hostile. His words to the department chair was, "I'm afraid of him".

We shared an office space, traveled to art exhibits together, I even offered to transport his artwork to exhibitions.

It was never in my soul to harm anyone nor him. What could make a person lie like this? Was it my age that intimidated him?

Was it how students gravitated towards me? Was it my skill as an artist? These were all triggers that he needed

to pull at me to kill my character in the eyes of the department. He feigned himself as a victim and I was the

aggressor and people bought into the sales pitch. Experience has taught me that desperate people will do anything to see your demise

because jealousy, covetousness and envy are the traits of a beast.

Carcinogen Personality

Look what Hitler did in Germany.

His negativity imbued the minds of the weak

to be a cancer to humanity. Seven million were

the receiving end of his cancerous agenda to

rule the world with an iron fist.

Take a step back and notice the picture I am painting.

Negative people are like cancer.

They seek to destroy people and progress.

They hate their outlook on life, and thrive to make others

feel negative like them. These folks aren't strangers, but those you

know. Some are even family members.

Avoid these people if you can and stay focused on your vision.

Don't tell them what you aspire to do because if you do,

they will inject it with cancer, killing your dreams.

I am carved from fire

It was turbulent times then. I was so confused and disoriented.

One, I couldn't bear the fact that you were dying.

You kept it a secret cause you knew I would worry.

You knew me best because if I knew, there's no

telling what I would have done. You were always a great decision maker.

My decisions caused me a lot of headache. I decided to

go on meds to help my racing thoughts, but it was all in vain.

I was coerced into thinking that something mentally was going on,

but I later found out that my thinking was normal. I stopped

the treatment which caused me merciless pain. 5 years of insomnia

added more trouble and agony. It only added to my stress as well

as yours because you loved me. You were the only human being that stood by me

in those fiery trials when everyone else mocked me. Unfortunately, your journey ended.

I was forced to continue it alone. At first, you and I couldn't understand the process.

The misfortune and ridicule were tumultuous. I was overlooked while others got ahead.

I played by the rules, but I still was handed the bad end of the stick.

I wish you were here to see me now. I'm still standing, but every now and then I have

some hang ups. God guided me through the fiery trials like a potter who puts his pottery into a kiln.

What you witnessed were the trials that molded me into the man that I am today.

These restraints are preparing me for the vision I saw. A vision that will someday manifest.

If you can endure the pain and ridicule in your adversity, the finished results are priceless.

Clogged Arteries: A Self-Portrait

I should've listened to the wiscom given to me about users.

My mom warned me, but my innocence blinded my eyes.

She tried to keep me from the spiders' web,

but before I decided to listen, I was already entangled.

I was the insect entrapped while they anticipated

to drain me of my accomplishments. I manage to get loose before

they went for the jugular vein.

Drowning your talent

Evil communications will rearrange
your behavior. A talented person with dreams
around an unclean atmosphere is destined for disaster
like Kensington Beach and Tioga in Philly, a den
of drowned talent.

Unclean spirits are very wise about life.
Its' been that way since the dawn of time.
Their mission has been to seek and destroy
by any means. That's why they introduced vices.
They know vices can destroy, and can suffocate your intelligence.
Vices make you dysfunctional and lethargic
eventually destroying mind, body and soul.

Nightmare

Abbadon visited me in the night. I was sound asleep
when he slithered his way into my room. Its
nothing new, his tricks haven't changed. His mission
is to intimidate like a mob enforcer who wants his pay.

I was laying down in my bed with my face turned toward the wall.
I felt a presence unlike anything I experienced. I turned
around and saw an image blacker than the darkness of the universe.
His height was over 7ft tall. He had no eyes or a mouth
just a shape of a man in the form of a Black cloud.
All I can do was stare. His gaze was like a dagger in
the heart, his hate was worse than fire. Standing next to my bed, he lifted
his right hand up with his fingers splayed open and palm facing me.
He stood there by my bed for minutes stiff like a stone.
I couldn't believe I was seeing this, but it was real.

The right hand is now clinched like a fist. When he clinched it,
it felt like a serpent coiled around me squeezing me tight until
I couldn't breathe. I was unconscious, but could feel the tightness.
Fearful, I called on that wonderful name and that old serpent
disappeared into the night.

The Ears

The sixth day of creation was a wonderful

day. A creature with the ability to speak and hear was born.

Formed and fashioned with sinews, bones and extremities to utilize

on earth, he was the image of uprightness. He was king of planet earth.

His counterpart was pulled from his side. She would bring death to

humanity because of one of her senses.

The ears are given to mankind to hear and process speech.

As a result of sin spiritual deafness entered the world.

It stopped the ears of man and woman causing a great woe on earth.

Like a table with erect dominoes that took hours of laborious dedication to install

someone bumps the table on purpose and one by one the dominoes fell.

Since that day, after Adam and Eve's transgression,

mankind fell like dominoes.

Coneheads

A cold winter day in Alabama, a festival in front of the state capital ensued. Dexter Avenue Baptist church is in clear view. Cheering hands and parade participants all in harmony marching in a syncopated rhythm until the last group entered the parade. It went from cheering to booing. What's all the commotion about I thought? As the group got closer the booing intensified. Making my way through the crowd, now I see why it went from happy to angry. Draped in disgrace in all kinds of colors. Their heads are conical with only their eyeballs visible. A symbol of pride and power to the scornful, but a symbol of genocide to the masses.

Wormwood and Gall

Hate for the opposite race isn't going grant us peace.

The commandments say we must love regardless of what was done.

To love a murderer I admit, is difficult to accomplish, but it must be done in order

to be at peace and good terms with GOD.

The Christian journey is all about denying yourself, and

doing what you normally wouldn't do.

We have tendencies to be revengeful taking matters in

our own hands which only causes more damage.

I see this emotion in racism and bigotry in the world…. Especially in America.

I must admit, forgiveness is a strong and bitter drink, but

you have to drink it all.

Failure

My teaching experience at a HBCU in Georgia was a horrible experience. I thought I failed.

The unprofessionalism was indescribable, but I manage to endure it.

10 years have passed since I was released from that campus prison.

It was not a place to grow spiritually, nor professionally.

People were content. No one was ambitious and wanted to strive for more.

So, what I thought was failure was really my protection.

False Accusers

In eighth grade myself, and a classmate was caught in a scandal.

The girl who hated my friend was mischievous and wanted him to get in trouble.

So, she devised a plan to falsely accuse him.

She approached me, and like an idiot I went along

with the story to destroy his character. My dad would have turned in his grave.

We approached the principal office and standing there we told lies.

Being a preacher's kid, I was evil, and weak to be swindled this way.

The principal saw through the lies like a clear glass jar. Because of our chicanery,

and my betrayal the principal suspended me and the girl for 3 days during

the week of Christmas Break.

Famine

The vices I struggle with are certainly causing a conflict in me.

These vices have become idols in my life.

They have certainly distorted my outlook, and dedication

in living righteous because my heart is swaddled in them.

They have become obstacles that I find hard to climb over.

The vices deprive my soul of proper spiritual nutrition

like photosynthesis to the flower.

We are plants of various hues and forms seeking

essentials from GOD to grow spiritually. What prevents

our spiritual growth are the vices we cling to which starves' our

souls to grow in peace and love.

Fire

I was created for a specific purpose.

My job is to warm, cleanse, to light and consume.

My age is ancient, so I have great wisdom. I was sent

to destroy kingdoms, plagued countries by my heat.

I was also made to kill humans, so when you see me don't take me lightly.

My results after I'm finished can be seen from miles away.

Smoke is my cousin and ashes are my children.

I have my own personality. I can comply or be stubborn, so I'm nothing to play with.

Humans have had an infatuation with me in the past, present and I see it coming in the future.

They even have professions named after me and crimes attached to my name.

Pyromaniacs and arsonist love to play with me.

Matches, aerosol sprays and gases are elements that make me tick, and

if there not careful, I can lose control and erase their existence like Sodom and Gomorrah.

Media is the cause for my body count.

I've been abuse and misused for Aeon's.

They promote me as toy by showing experiments

and tricks. My lethalness is taken for granted just ask my victims.

There's a side of me that can't be quenched.

During the exodus, I was sent to be a light to Israel.

I consumed sacrifices on the altar before the patriarchs.

I destroyed Aaron's sons for mishandling me.

I even appeared to their uncle in a burning bush.

There's one more part to me that's divine, but dreadful.

I have an eternal destination reserved for the disobedient.

Forgiveness

To become acquainted with backbiting and slander is

the life of the righteous. Your name is the topic of discussion with

unspeakable shame. I cannot express to you how many times I've

been in situations like this. False accusations and

calumny, bound me to a column and pierced me with arrows

like Andrea Mantegna's painting, The Martyrdom of Saint Sabastian.

Your religion is what initiated the public execution. Your purest attitude

toward scripture makes you profane in the eyes

of the unlearned. The word is out that you're in a religious

cult, now you wonder why when you call people or stop by there

homes, and no one answers the phone or door.

Now bear this in mind, all of this isn't done by outsiders,

but those of the same kindred.

Grave Diggers

Do you know grave diggers? Not those who work at a cemetery, but worthless people who have a mind to destroy your character in the eyes of people. They work in unison to dig a pit, so they can bury your name and accomplishments.

Grave diggers are unproductive creatures that hate progress. Sometimes you don't know who they are because they are camouflaged, but let something bad happen to you then they will stick out like a black rose amidst a bouquet of red roses.

So, if you know grave diggers don't call any names. Just know that there plans and schemes will bury them.

Grip

I

Sophomore year in school conversations sparked the interest.

Thoughts of trying it infested your mind

which later incited the desire.

II

That dreadful day arrived

when you gave into the thought.

It over takes your body like demoniac.

III

Righteous Job fought the grip. He didn't allow his circumstances to affect his faith. Even though his wife urged him to leave God he withstood her and rebuke her evil words. There will be times where you will have to choose like Job did. A lesson from his trial shows us that our integrity must always outweigh fleshly desires.

Hidden Agenda: A message to the Gullible

I

Beware of those who pretend to be supportive.

You trust because of smiling faces, but underneath

it's a corpse. I was blind to there

chicanery because of my inexperience with life.

For 20 plus years, I thought these so-called friends would

keep me out of danger. They were retired teachers in the school system,

and knew the atmosphere I was getting into, so they put me in a difficult situation

where I almost lost my freedom.

They suggested that I be a substitute teacher something I didn't want to do, but since

they were older and had experience, I decided to go ahead and try.

I should have stuck with my intuition, but my financial situation was terrible.

I regret the decision I made to become a substitute teacher

because this memory is still a nightmare.

II

I didn't tolerate foolishness. What you got away with

with your other teachers, wasn't going to happen with me.

Most kids didn't have a male figure at home, so to see one who wasn't

afraid of them created a hostile environment.

III

I didn't back down, and if you thought of putting your hands on me you can rest assure I manhandled you.

IV

Blessed are your eyes that you can see.

I wished I saw their deception sooner, but it made me more wise

to write this message to you.

Deceptive people are walking graves inwardly who

seek to devour those whose eyes are closed to their deceit.

I will rise

I

In an evil generation where standards are a myth endure the pain
and remember that one day you will rise.
You may be falsely accused or your character assassinated.
You may be scorned and suffer cruel mocking's.
You may see parents succumb to their disease like I saw when I was young and
when I became a man.

II

When I witness the death of my mom, I was in pitch black darkness.
It was like being locked in an empty closet.
To see her lifeless body lying there cold as ice on a hospital bed
I thought it wasn't real. I picked up her arm hoping she would stop playing
and hold it up on her own, but it fell down limped.

III

This body is just a house for the soul. Christ Jesus said that
those who've died will rise again.

In the midst of fire

My first job was a grocery clerk at a store. I was in the

10th grade. It was ritual in my household

that everyone got a job while they were in high school.

Bills needed to be paid and groceries needed to be bought.

I didn't know that the store manager was racist though.

His views towards black people was the bigoted fashion.

Every black is a nigger. He was a dangerous person because

he would smile in your face, but say negative things about you behind your back.

For some reason he picked on me. He always had something to say.

 If I wasn't smiling he asked, "Why do you look like that?"

If I wasn't moving fast enough he always addressed me in

a crowd of people for my slow movements. He made it his effort to embarrass me in front

of my co-workers and customers. One day it was the last straw. I got home from school to change into

my work clothes. I only worked about 3 miles away from my house,

so, my mom didn't have to drive very long to drop me off. It was an all

white Lincoln continental town car with plush velvet burgundy seats. When you drove

off, it would make a winding sound. My mom loved that car,

and so, did I. We get to the store and I told her goodbye, she said,

"I'll pick you up at 9pm." Boy was I in for it when I got inside the store.

I put my red apron on and started bagging groceries. He called my name

and asked if I could go find a product on the isle for him. His tone

had an attitude with it. I knew that this was not going to be a good day.

I found the product for him and handed it to him. I guess he thought

I couldn't find it. Time passed and I continued to bag groceries, he called me to his office

and told me to go home. I asked why? But he ignored me. I only been at work for 2 hours.

I called home and told her the news. My mom was enraged. She gets to my job and told me

"Give me your apron and wait in the car". I knew then it was serious trouble for the manager. The store was packed. Furious,

she rushed inside to find him standing in front of the store monitoring employees, and

with all her might, she balls the red apron up and throws it in his face, and pointed her finger at him and yelled, "You're a racist."

She storms out the store. The whole store came to a stand-still while his face turned red with embarrassment.

He never saw it coming. I quit that day.

(27)

Isolated

Isolation is an atmosphere you can render praise

and worship to develop a closeness with GOD.

A place of focus, silence and peace which everybody needs.

Especially in these times of racial tension

and police brutality which has everyone on edge.

I think its planned to create pandemonium. A dress rehearsal to usher

in a one world government for the beast.

Those creating the chaos wants the world

to bow to the scarlet red dragon that old serpent.

He needs isolation to get into your head to coerce you to worship him.

So, remember when you're isolated be mindful

that the accuser is right next to you creeping his way into your mind with

negative thoughts and confusion.

Jewels

Television has certainly misconstrued the value of jewels.

They advertise it as something monetary.

True jewels are not monetary, but priceless.

Jewels is not what you wear on your body.

It's not what you make in a factory.

It's not what you collect in museums and homes,

but wisdom on how to survive.

Gun Ptah

I

An idol that was made by hands of men

these handheld destroyers revolutionized warfare.

The natives in the Americas couldn't manage to withstand it,

especially with spears and arrows while the conquistadors

went mayhem.

II

A difficult weapon to obtain is now accessible like a phone.

You don't have to go to a pawn shop to buy one. You

can buy them on the street or find one on a playground.

III.

These idols have infiltrated the world.

Incarcerations levels are high, the slain have tipped the scales.

Street soldiers keep their trust in them because the

say it protects them. This is only pseudo trust and commitment.

These instruments of cruelty jam and misfire, oftentimes

killing those who hold them.

IV

My High school wrestling coach had many of them.

He was a U.S. marine. He cleaned them like they were part of

his body. These idols were human to him and he knew the power

they possessed because he studied them.

V

His cancer came back. A pseudo relationship with an already married woman took him to the cleaners and took all his money and left town. Military benefits are what drew her to him. It all happened in a small town in West Florida. Neighbors saw him pace up and down the street in front of his house. After hours of pacing he went to his patio and sat in his chair. He opened his mouth and brains went everywhere.

A Cold Heart

I

A fun day at school at least you thought.

A man with a white van is parked out front.

He's waiting inside for the next victim

like a lion who waits for the next gazelle.

Just 6 years old and full of energy. He drew a picture

of you and him eager to show you his masterpiece

he created in art class.

II

The excitement came to an end.

He lured him with a lollipop. The door closed behind him like

an alligator who clamps down on his recent kill.

III

Days go by and amber alerts are sent out on news stations and

radio networks. No traces of the child. Insomnia envelops

you like fog. All this event seems unreal.

IV

On Halloween a body of the small child was found.

Neighbors complained about a foul smell coming from a trailer.

The coroner's office enters and discovers a

decomposing body of a child with bloody underwear,

and a drawing next to them. The body bears a
birth mark that you recognize.

Swallow Your Pride

I

Just because you're older doesn't mean you know more.

Age does not prove that you have wisdom, but it is God who determines

whose wise and it is he who gives wisdom.

II

You say that young people have more advantages and haven't

experienced hardships, but you had both parents in their prime

whereas, I had one parent who was 63 years old when I graduated high school.

III

My first car was bought with lawsuit money I won due to

a racial profiling incident that happened to me

at a shopping mall when I was 17 years old, whereas your

parents bought your first car.

IV

The Three Hebrews brothers who refused to worship the Babylonian god

were young when they were thrown in a fiery furnace, Daniel was young when he was

thrown in a den of Lions, and righteous David was young when he slew Goliath.

So, if you think age is the only element of wisdom and experience you are certainly mistaken,

I hope these words will help you attain humility.

Light equals Knowledge

Eyes open and not open the pit is dark and dismal.

True light lights the paths of souls and keep you out of shackles.

Eyes open and not open the pit is dark and dismal.

True light lights your path for those who are willing to listen.

They were many before you who were on the same course, but they stop their ears from hearing truth. A person or thing won them over, and caused them to let go of knowledge.

A Smile

A smile is unique, and you never know its purpose.

Some people smile when they're happy,

some smile in pain, some smile for laughter

or some smile to masks their evil intentions.

I met these type people in my life.

I was unaware that some people don't frown

when they have an evil motive, but are friendly and

cordial.

Nay-sayers

Naysayers drain your spirit like vampires. Beware of them they could be people you know hiding their deception with smiles and laughter. They pretend to be supportive of your dreams, but behind your back they speak evil of your confidence. To find out if someone is a naysayer allow adversity and trouble to happen in your life.

Pig Slop

I

I returned to graduate school to pursue a second master's degree

in Fine Arts. My decision to return to school was to make myself

more valuable in the job market. It was the perfect time to return because

my combined credit from my previous degree cut my M.F.A Program

from 2 years to 1 year.

II

My tenure there wasn't the best experience. To me it was mediocrity because

I felt as though I didn't receive the full amount of commitment from my professors.

My experience was like traveling on a hiking trip without the necessities needed to

maintain myself in the wilderness like a compass and Poison ivy kit.

III

I stood 6'2 265 pounds. I had an athletic physic because of my college football

career. I wasn't your typical art student. Students would ask security if I was a

student. The stereotypes became a norm, so I was already prepared to answer with student

ID in hand.

IV

The absence and mediocrity I felt during my program I would asked myself questions internally.

Did my athletic physic intimidate my professors? Were they afraid to critique my work

because of it? Was it a clique they formed only to help students they felt safe around?

V

I later found out from a classmate who overheard a conversation

from our professors about me. The conclusion was that they were intimidated by me

and feared that if they had the slightest criticism about my artwork

that I would be violent with them. Their plan was to push me along

without any confrontation.

(36)

Chained Down

I

Negative experiences can haunt you.

Classmates teased you because of your physical features.

A birth mark, gaped teeth, good grades, bifocals, freckles, your shoes,

clothing, or even speaking evil about your family.

II

These types interactions can cause a person to go insane.

You can sink into depression or possibly commit suicide if you allow it.

It sounds like a fable, but bullying is real. I have experienced it and certainly

seen others go through it. Some students don't perform well academically because

they don't want to stand out amongst their peers and fear of being bullied.

III

These experiences can imprison your production in life.

You can either let it control you and keep you imprisoned or use it as motivation to reach

your goals. You were made to be useful and not useless, so don't let

bad experiences chain down your progress.

Reckless Energy

Someone wanted to be a bootleg manicurist

that nearly chopped off their finger.

I was at work when it happened.

When I got home, her hand was wrapped in a gauze like a boxing glove.

Furious, I quenched my anger like a geyser.

On a hot summer in July, something so menial triggered

the explosion. I suggested an alternative that could have prevented

the error, but was greeted with unkind words. It triggered a side of me

I did not know existed. In rage, I put my hands on them and threw them

to the floor. It was all waisted energy spent on the mundane

when I could have just walked away.

Regret

Regret isn't racist nor male or female chauvinistic. It

affects all humanity. It certainly happened to me when I was

in high school. One of my teammates failed his writing portion of the

high school graduation test. I never forgot how I laughed at him for failing,

but little did I know that I would reap what I sowed.

In return for my stupidity of laughing at him, I failed it.

The feeling I felt of making fun of him was comparable

to a perfect pass thrown from the quarterback for the

game winning touchdown that goes right through my hands.

All week I rehearsed the play, which I never dropped a pass at practice.

Remote Control

Class, beauty and wealth are tools used to control.
Manipulating minds of the weak, the ones who are
easily misled. Selling your soul isn't just money.
It can be a person that can take your soul. Your lust overtakes
your common sense that caused you to
overlook their ulterior motives. Their outward appearance made
you deny and turn on those who love you. For them this is
entertainment, but disappointment to those
who genuinely care for you. A manipulative person
loves control and use people who are gullible.

Revenge

Why hold grudges against doubters?

It won't help you nor is it profitable to your

spiritual development. All it does is cause

you stress, anguish and loathness towards them

which are fruits that are not allowed in the kingdom of GOD.

While you're irritated they go along with there

lives as usual. Are you willing to give them this power?

The greatest revenge you can ever do is to be successful

in the very thing they didn't believe in. They are now forced

to eat their doubting words and swallow them like nails.

Revolving Door

In and out of relationships are unhealthy to the soul.

It's like looking at a beautiful piece of Dale Chihuly

glass sculpture that's filled with excrement.

When you act this way, you are not the only one affected,

but those who are close to you are hurting as well.

Having different mates in and out of your life

looks bad. In their eyes you look like a revolving door.

Are you that desperate to find a companion to fill a void

that only belongs to GOD? Will you continue to go through mental and physical abuse?

Will you continue to take gifts as an apology?

You are much more valuable than objects and deserve better. Just remember,

your life doesn't have to be a revolving door.

Sinister Zeitgeist

The streets of America are reminiscent of
Jackson Pollock *Drip paintings.* Blood
and gore replaced the paint. A conversation with
your children usually were about college, but now
parents are having dialogue with their sons on how
to stay alive.

Black rings and black figures on shooting targets are dress rehearsal
of what we are experiencing on the streets of America.
The woes of police brutality are the unholy spirit of our times.

Someday the stone will roll away

Life brings terrible experiences that alter your life.

The hurt it causes is so tremendous that

it takes your desire and hope away. Your faith

weakens and doubt settles in your soul.

The stones in your life are bad habits or people.

The stronghold it has on you is, so forceful that it cast

a shadow over your body. It's now dangerous to take

one step because you don't know how close to the cliff you are.

When you're in this dilemma prayer and faith will clear

any stones that impede your future.

Werewolves

Werewolves are not fiction, but are real.

During the 1920's and 30's a werewolf roamed the streets of New York's Wisteria district. An old innocent looking man terrorized with so much villainy and barbarism that people were afraid to walk the streets.

His victims were young boys and girls.

They didn't pose a threat because he could overpower them.

With his cold-blooded heart he strangled, molested and cannibalized them for no reason just for ecstasy and erotic pleasure. By eating the flesh of these children he felt a sense of relief like a masochist.

Like a Francisco de Goya painting, *Saturn Devouring his children* he literal took this picture to heart and reenacted it in real life.

His serial rampage of innocent children ended in an electric chair.

Star Gazer

Created by GOD for farming and maritime they
were worshipped as gods by foolish men and
women thousands of years ago.
With evil intent, and tainted minds they made lifeless images
with their hands to draw away people to worship in vain.
Their conduct has trickled down thousands of years later where
people still worship idols. As dress rehearsal, political leaders, preachers
are partaking in satanic rituals to draw away millions to
take the mark of the beast using the prosperity plan as a red carpet.

Stepping Stones: A Homage to Coach Rock

My college football coach wasn't the easiest

to work with. He was a local legacy in Indiana.

He was a Notre Dame athlete, and his father was a professional

football player and a Marine. Apples don't fall to far from the tree.

His tough demeanor came off very aggressive and

no one liked it. Not even me in the beginning.

The reason people disliked liked him was his brutal honesty.

If you didn't perform he will tell you in your face

whether you liked it or not.

As I matured, I later realized that his meanness

was a technique. He wanted the best out of you, so

if he had to talk and treat you mean that's what he

did. He would say, "After football men, you don't 'want

any regrets when you hang up the cleats, so leave it all

out on the field... play every play like it's your last".

People are not sincere

Seeing your situation and despair they feigned their hospitality because in their hearts lay deceit.
They cloak themselves in humility and charity. They play on your emotions because they know you're in a fragile mind frame.
The frustration, and desperation weakens your defense.

I was in a situation like this which took three years to recover from it.
False people consoled me only to use what they did for me as leverage. Since they helped me financially, they thought they could speak and treat me disrespectfully as they desired.

If you're this type of person that help people and use your finances as tool to manipulate and oppress them while they are weak, then keep what you have to offer because you are not genuine.

Taking a Stand for Truth

I was led by a false prophet who deceived me.

I thought Christmas was the birthday of our messiah Jesus

Christ, but to find out that it was not, is a divine act to save my soul.

A true apostle was sent to open my eyes and see it was all a lie.

In actuality, it was a day set aside by Rome to honor

their pagan god whose name is Saturn. The origin

of putting gifts under a tree symbolize bringing offerings

to the god Saturn. This day is simply a satanic ritual that

people are unaware of because Saturn is another name

for Satan. At first, no one bought into it, but cunning set in.

To get people to go along they substituted the name Saturn

with Jesus and that's how billions of followers bought into the witchcraft.

Little do they know that December 25th is a day set aside by Rome

to worship Satan. It is true that people perish by a lack of knowledge.

Jeremiah Chapter 10 verses 1-4 gives me confidence

that I am on the right path of salvation.

To this day, I no longer celebrate Christmas.

My family and some acquaintances think I'm in a religious cult.

Because of my stability and integrity, I am being ostracized for it.

When you take a stand for truth, people will certainly think the most

outrageous things about you because the heart is deep and desperately wicked.

So, when you take a stand for truth don't be shocked who turns on you.

The Abyss

When your freedom is taken away from you

are you still confident in your belief?

Will you still be the man or woman of faith

if you're stricken with an illness, lose a spouse, child

or lose a job?

Adversity and tribulation are an abyss. It is a place

of discomfort, pain and anguish. Not all can survive its

darkness and isolation, so if you're still alive there is hope.

I was stripped of my necessities and thrown into an abyss

over 5 years ago. In darkness it's difficult to see, so your

ears are important when vision is impaired.

Through hearing, I discovered that people I thought were

supportive actually enjoyed seeing me in the abyss, so when

you're in your abyss be attentive to words.

58

About the Author

Charles Parham was born and raised in Columbus, Georgia as the youngest of eleven children. Though his early years were filled with much turmoil, that being centered on the untimely death of his father, these years were also the central influence in his artwork.

It was only natural that later in life, Charles would meet great success as an illustrator – even having one of his children book designs to be accepted in an international competition. In the 15th Annual Teatrio Competition entitled, *"Dodgeball"*, Charles was one of 30 finalists to represent the Savannah College of Art and Design in Italy in 2009. It wasn't long before his passion for uninhibited expression led him to painting.

It was just recently that Charles was led to poetry. After suffering unemployment for almost three years, and the tragedy of losing his mother to kidney disease, Charles found poetry as an outlet to express his faith and pain. Charles used the turmoil he encountered not as a way to lash out at his enemies, but to empower his faith by writing poetry that would help inspire, motivate and inform the reader that there is hope. Charles expresses that his poetry is not written for entertainment, but is written for those who are experiencing hardships, chaos and doubt. He says that he was once wounded by these emotions, but his faith in GOD pulled him from the muck and mire, and inspired him to write this book.

WARERESOURCES AND PUBLISHING WE ARE AN
ALL IN ONE, ONE STOP PUBLISHING COMPANY!!!!

W.R.P. is a modest but skilful and knowledgeable Christian Publishing Company. We specialize in getting authors into print. We embrace and guide each author like a member of our family. We treat you fairly and recognize the importance of building a lasting relationship with you as an author. Join us in the walk to promote prosperity along with the message of encouragement and peace. Be one of the authors we transform and prepare for the world of information and books.

FEEL FREE TO CONTACT US@
www.wareresources.com
1-800-469-4850 EXT. 2

Ware Resources and Publishing
You Start and Finish With Us!

www.ingramcontent.com/pod-product-compliance
Lightning Source LLC
LaVergne TN
LVHW010616070526
838199LV00063BA/5167